►Special Days◄

Easter

Pam Robson

HODDER
Wayland

An imprint of Hodder Children's Books

►Special Days◄

Bonfire Night
Christmas
Easter
May Day
Mother's Day
Poppy Day

Editor: Liz Gogerly
Photo stylist: Gina Brown
Series design: Kate Buxton
Book designer: Joyce Chester
Illustrator: Chris Molan
Illustrator (pancake recipe): Tony de Saulles
Consultants: Jacqui Harrison and Rhona Perry of Stepping Stones

First published in 1999 by Wayland Publishers Limited
This paperback edition published in 2002 by Hodder Wayland,
an imprint of Hodder Children's Books

British Library Cataloguing in Publication Data
Robson, Pam
Easter. – (Special Days)
1. Easter – Juvenile literature
I. Title
394.2'667

ISBN 0 7502 4392 9

Typeset in England by Joyce Chester
Printed in Hong Kong

Picture Acknowledgements
The publishers would like to thank the following for allowing us to reproduce their pictures:
AKG 13; Bridgeman Art Library 12; Chapel Studios/Zul *cover* (main), 4; Mary Evans 21 (bottom), 29; Eye Ubiquitous *cover*
(background), 5 (bottom); Hulton Getty 19, 26; Popperfoto 17 (top), 27 (top), (bottom), 30; Tony Stone 5, (top) 6, 21 (top); Topham
Picturepoint 10, 15, 20; Wayland/Rupert Horrox 8/National Gallery 18.

Contents

When is Easter?

Spring begins on 21st March. Easter comes soon after the first day of spring. Easter is the most important festival for Christians. They remember the last week of Jesus' life. On Easter Day they celebrate because they remember how Jesus rose from the dead.

▼ Children have fun on Easter Sunday looking for Easter eggs in the garden.

▲ Yellow daffodils flower again once spring arrives.

▲ New life begins. Lambs play in the fields.

Spring and Easter have always gone together. A long time ago there was a goddess of spring called Eastre. In northern Europe there was a spring festival called Ostara.

New life in spring

During the cold winter, nature is asleep. But when spring arrives the plants and animals wake. Green shoots push up through the brown earth. Birds build their nests and lay their eggs. Eggs and new life are part of Easter.

▲ Eggs are symbols of new life. Everyone looks forward to spring when fluffy yellow chicks hatch from their eggs.

An old Chinese story tells us that the
world comes from a big egg. Pian ku,
a giant, hatches from an egg. The top
of the egg becomes the sky and the
bottom becomes the earth.

▼ Pian ku hatches from
the enormous egg.

Fun before Easter

Before Easter arrives there has always been a quiet time called Lent. But, in February, before Lent begins, everyone has fun.

This is carnival time in many countries. The word 'carnival' means 'goodbye to meat'. Long ago Christians did not eat meat or fat at this time.

◀ Many years ago in Venice, in Italy, people dressed up and wore masks during carnival. People all over the world still wear fancy dress at this time.

Making pancakes

Carnival time ends on Shrove Tuesday or Pancake Day. A long time ago people feasted, to use up any meat, eggs, milk and flour, before Lent began.

Now we make pancakes.

▲ Earlier this century these ladies raced to their local church with their pancakes. It is still the tradition to have pancake races on Shrove Tuesday.

A pancake recipe

Ingredients:
100g plain flour
pinch of salt
1 egg
1/2 pint milk
vegetable oil

You will need:
a mixing bowl
a wooden spoon
a frying pan

What you do:

1. Sift the flour and salt into a bowl and add the egg. Slowly pour in a little of the milk and mix your ingredients gently with a wooden spoon until smooth. Add the rest of the milk, a little at a time, until the batter is creamy.

2. Ask a grown-up to heat the oil in the frying pan until hot. Pour in enough of the batter to make one pancake. Cook the pancake until it is brown on one side then toss the pancake to brown the other side.

3. Serve your pancake with lemon and sugar. Try other fillings, such as bananas, ice-cream and chocolate sauce.

The first day of Lent

Ash Wednesday is the first day of Lent. A long time ago Ash Wednesday was a day of fasting. Now, on this day, people give up luxuries, such as sweets and chocolate, for Lent. This means they try not to eat these foods for forty days!

▲ This picture shows a pretend battle between Carnival and Lent. Carnival is on the left and Lent is on the right.

12

During Lent Christians remember how Jesus once fasted for forty days. They also spend more time at prayer and reading the Bible.

▼ On this day it is traditional for Christians to have a cross marked on their heads with ash. This reminds them to feel sorry for the bad things they have done.

The Jewish spring festival

Passover is the Jewish spring festival. During Passover, Jews remember the story of how the Jewish people escaped from slavery in Egypt many thousands of years ago.

▼ At Passover time many Jewish families gather together to eat a special meal.

▲ Two thousand years ago Jesus
celebrated Passover with his friends.
This was to be their last meal together.

Jesus was Jewish and the story of Easter begins
when he goes to a Passover. Jesus travelled to a
Passover in a town called Jerusalem, in a country
then named Palestine.

Palm Sunday

Holy Week is the week leading up to Easter Day. Palm Sunday is the first day of Holy Week. This is when Jesus entered Jerusalem on a donkey. The people of Jerusalem were very excited. They waved palm branches to welcome him to their town.

▼ When Jesus rode into Jerusalem on a donkey this was the first Palm Sunday.

Christians now remember this day by decorating their churches with palm leaves. Small palm crosses are also given to everybody. In colder countries, where palm trees do not grow, pussy willow and catkins are sometimes gathered too.

▲ In Poland children sometimes wear straw hats like these on Palm Sunday.

17

Maundy Thursday

On Maundy Thursday we remember when Jesus washed the feet of his friends. He did this to show that all people are the same, whether they are kings or servants. Kings and queens used to wash the feet of twelve poor people on this day.

◀ Our Queen, Elizabeth II, gives special silver Maundy coins to old people in need on this day.

Some people did not like Jesus. They thought he was too popular. The next part of the Easter story is sad because Jesus was betrayed by one of his friends called Judas. Jesus was then arrested by his enemies and taken away.

◀ Judas shows the enemies who Jesus is.

Good Friday

The next day Jesus was crucified on a cross. Then his body was placed in a tomb.

◀ The crucifix, or the cross, is the symbol for Christianity.

We call this day Good Friday. It is the saddest day of Easter because we remember how Jesus suffered and died. In Germany this day is called Silent Friday.

In Victorian times hot cross buns were sold in the streets on Good Friday. ▼

People still eat hot cross buns. The cross reminds us of when Jesus was crucified. ▶

Easter is here!

After the sadness of Good Friday, Easter Day is a happy day. This is because people remember how Jesus rose from the dead – this is called the Resurrection. In many countries on Easter morning church bells ring to celebrate.

▶ Jesus came back to life on Easter Day and talked with his friends on the beach.

Christians celebrate Easter

Every year, on Easter Sunday, Christians attend church services to remind them of how Jesus came back to life. A special candle is lit, called the paschal candle.

On Ascension Day, forty days after Easter, Christians remember how Jesus rose up to heaven. Then the paschal candle is blown out.

▶ On Easter Sunday the paschal candle is lit and the church is filled with fresh spring flowers, such as daffodils.

Eggs go with Easter

Later on Easter Sunday, families and friends have fun. A long time ago people could not eat eggs during Lent. Of course, the hens did not stop laying eggs, so these eggs were decorated and given as gifts on Easter Sunday. Today we still paint eggs for fun, but we usually give chocolate eggs as gifts.

▲ These children lost their homes during the Second World War. It was hard to get chocolate then but these children are being given Easter eggs.

It is only 100 years since the first chocolate Easter eggs were made. At that time, they were made by hand but now they are made in factories, so they are cheaper.

▲ This huge chocolate Easter egg is made by hand.

Children enjoy playing games on Easter Sunday. These children are taking part in an egg and spoon race. ▶

More Easter fun

People like to wear new clothes on Easter Day. People all around the world enjoy special Easter parades. In New York there is an Easter bonnet parade.

▶ The first Easter bonnet parade was held in New York over 100 years ago, just after the American Civil War.

28

Easter is celebrated in many ways throughout the world. It is a special and important occasion for Christians. But it is also a time for everybody to have fun and enjoy their Easter eggs.

▼ People send special cards at Easter. This card is over 80 years old. It shows an Easter bunny, a rooster and a hen.

EASTER GREETING

29

Glossary

Betrayed   To be let down by a friend who tells an enemy your secrets or lies about you.

Celebrate   To remember a special day.

Crucified   To be nailed and bound to a large wooden cross and left to die.

Fasting   To go without food for a long time on purpose.

Festival   A time of celebration.

Parade   To march through the streets, sometimes in fancy dress.

Resurrection   The coming back to life of Jesus.

Symbol   A thing which reminds us of something else.

Tradition   A custom handed down year after year.

Victorian times   Over 100 years ago when Queen Victoria was queen of England.

Timeline

1250 BC   The Old Testament Bible story of the Exodus takes place. The Jews escape from slavery in Egypt. This event is still remembered at Passover time. BC stands for the words 'before Christ'. The Exodus happened a long time before Christ was born.

1 AD   AD stands for the words 'Anno Domini' which means 'the Year of our Lord'. It is the first year of the Christian calendar which begins when Christ is born.

30 AD   The Easter story happens in Jerusalem. Christ is crucified on Good Friday and comes to life again on Easter Day

1828   A way of making eating chocolate is invented.

1877   The wife of President Madison of the USA introduces egg rolling on the lawn of the White House in Washington.

1880   The Easter Bonnet Parade, in Madison Avenue, New York, becomes a tradition. Starts after the American Civil War, to promote the sale of hats.

1905   Cadburys make dairy milk chocolate for the first time.

Further information

Books to Read

The Easter Story by Heather Amery (Usborne Books, 1999)

Easter by Philip Sauvain (Wayland, 1997)

Easter by Catherine Chambers (Evans, 1998)

A Feast of Festivals by Jan Thompson (Heinemann, 1995)

Index